FRUITION

DEFINING MOMENTS THAT ALTER THE
TRAJECTORY OF YOUR ACTUALIZED
PURPOSE

DR. KAMILAH M. G. ELLIS

FOREWORD BY:
DR. DONNA M. HUNTER

FRUITION

Copyright © 2024 by Kamilah Ellis

ISBN: 979-8-218-97895-2

www.getfruitionconsulting.com

DEDICATION

To my precious babies, Kristopher and Karrington. I pray that you will grow to be all, do all, and have all that God wants you to be, do, and have. May you experience holy boldness and confidence in Christ to walk in the fullness of your calling; and may you remain in the center of Christ's perfect will for your lives, to dwell in the fruition of your purpose. Mommy loves you, Lovey and Sweetles!!! I love you with all of my heart, every single part of me, and every fiber of my being. I will always be proud of you, and I will always believe in you!

ACKNOWLEDGEMENTS

I have been so blessed to have many family members, friends and loved ones who have supported me in this endeavor. I would like to express my perpetual gratitude to the following individuals:

To my husband, Greg, thank you for supporting me and encouraging me in every single ministerial pursuit of passion that I have to touch the lives of others in the various ways that God has blessed me to be gifted in.

To my immediate family, my parents, my siblings, my siblings-in-love, and my nieces and nephews, thank you for your kindness, compassion, understanding of my peculiar anointing, and love. I love each of you with all of my heart.

To my senior pastors, Bishop Dr. E. John E. Crocker and Pastor Janielle Crocker, I thank you for believing in me, for loving me, truly understanding me, and pushing me to do what God has charged me to do. I love you both tremendously, my brother and sister in Christ and my good friends!

To my spiritual parents, Senior Pastor Emeritus, Bishop Dr. John Crocker and Pastor Emerita Theresa Crocker, thank you for my spiritual and ministerial upbringing, and for loving me unconditionally since I was a little girl. Also, thank you for blessing me with my favorite Bible when I was in high school, which is featured on the front cover of this book! This Bible has traveled with me from places I have lived… to Oklahoma and back, California and back, and is a treasured keepsake that not only nourishes my spirit, but also fills my heart with precious memories of where my Christian walk began. I will always love and cherish you both!

To my brother and sister in Christ, Youth Pastor John C. Harris, Jr. and Glory Harris (owner of *Glorious Images*, my headshots photographer extraordinaire and amazing book cover designer), thank you for your support and love for our family! We love you guys!

Last, but certainly not least, to my good friend and sister in Christ, Dr. Donna Marie Hunter, thank you for your friendship, for your love and for your support in this project.

I am so grateful for all of our Azusa Pacific doctoral cohort memories in and out of class…the ups and the downs, the laughs, the tears, the victories and defeats, and everything in between! Thank you for always being a constant supporter of mine, an encourager, a lovely example for others, a dream builder and an uplifter. You are amazing, my sister-friend! I praise God with you for the great things that He is continuing to do in your life, and I know that your best is yet to come! Many blessings to you and your family, and much love always!

TABLE OF CONTENTS

FOREWORD

In the journey of faith, we often find ourselves navigating through a myriad of experiences, each shaping our understanding of God and His purposes for our lives. At times, we are buoyed by moments of clarity and spiritual growth, feeling as though we are walking in step with God's divine plan. Yet, there are moments when we encounter roadblocks—challenges that shake the very foundations of our faith and leave us questioning our path.

For some of us, these roadblocks manifest as disappointments, feelings of inadequacy, or a sense of dejection that seems to cloud our vision of God's promises. We yearn to grow in our relationship with Him, to be used by Him in ways that bring glory to His name, yet we find ourselves hindered by doubt and fear.

But amidst the ebb and flow of our spiritual journey, there is a constant, an unwavering truth that we can cling to: we are children of God, loved deeply and intimately by the Creator of the universe. In the midst of uncertainty, His love remains steadfast, His purposes unshakeable.

This book is a beacon of hope, a guide for those who seek to navigate the complexities of their Christian walk with courage and perseverance. Whether you find yourself facing roadblocks that threaten to derail your faith or grappling with feelings of inadequacy that hinder your growth, know this— God is with you.

Through the pages of this book, may you be encouraged to press on, to stir up the spiritual gifts within you, and to boldly pursue the calling that God has placed upon your life. May you find solace in the knowledge that you are not alone, that countless others have walked this path before you, and that together, as a community of believers, we can overcome every obstacle that stands in our way.

So, dear reader, be not dismayed. For though the road may be long and the journey arduous, we walk not in our own strength but in the power of the One who has called us.

May this book serve as a reminder of His faithfulness and a catalyst for transformation in your life.

In His Grace,

Dr. Donna Marie Hunter

PREFACE

At the time of writing this book about a year ago, there were various things in my life that were different than they are now, as you begin reading through these pages. When I started writing, I was working at a different job, my children were in different grade levels, my marriage has been through various phases, and *both* of my parents were still with me in this earthly realm, among other nuances to life.

As it were, my Daddy had gone through various health challenges over the years, which progressively got worse, to the point of an unexpected, serious incurable illness. Devastatingly, he passed away a few months before the publication of my book.

I was his Baby Girl and he was my Daddy.. a constant consistent and comforting presence in my life. He was always so proud of me, as he was proud of all four of us; and I know that he would have been so proud of me publishing this book. His legacy lives on through each of us and although my Daddy is not here to see the continued fruit of his labor on earth, I take great joy and comfort in knowing that he was a beautiful example for us all. He loved the Lord Jesus Christ with all of his heart, and my Dad left this life after having walked in the fruition of his purpose. He was an inspiration to many, and I pray that this book inspires each of you to do likewise!

INTRODUCTION

Have you ever been riding in the car and noticed on the side of the road a sign with a picture of a big, beautiful building, and a caption that says, "Coming Soon"? Perhaps it is a new shopping center, entertainment complex, or even an office building! In that fleeting moment, you hope that whatever the building will be, it will suit y*our* own needs or meet your wishes. Whether or not the building will be a new movie theater, restaurant, medical center, or grocery store, one thing is for certain. There is usually *something* that comes up which will either delay the construction or alter the original design, if not do both.

Generally, in our twenties and teens (sometimes even younger), we begin to envision what our future might look like as we come to discover things that we are good at, and passionately develop our own likes and interests. Some people are blessed to discover their purpose at an early age, cultivate their skill sets, and receive continual opportunities to stir up their spiritual gifts! Similarly, it is possible for the erection of a new building to be done seamlessly: free of modifications and delays. What a relief when the building is completed on schedule without any mishaps! That is, I am sure, a truly remarkable experience!

However, if you are like me, the construction of *your* proverbial "building" might have gone through delays and alterations. Our buildings are still under construction. Some buildings might be finished and open for business, only requiring occasional maintenance, while other buildings are still a work in progress.

The Prophet Nehemiah was saddened by the destruction and ruin of the walls of Jerusalem. So he received special dispensation from King Artexertes to go and rebuild the wall so that Jerusalem could be restored and habitable again by the Israelites. Sometimes, we experience the vicissitudes of life, which can cause temporary damage to the "building," but through breakthrough, repentance, restoration and faith, we can set our mind to build ourselves up and go on in the name of the Lord.

God gave Nehemiah very specific detailed instructions on how to go about rebuilding the walls of Jerusalem. Of course, any time you start doing something for the Lord, the devil gets mad and you become faced with opposition. Even though Nehemiah came with a letter of permission from the king, and some of the king's soldiers, the governor, Sanballat and his servant Tobiah took personal offense with Nehemiah's intention to restore Jerusalem. They plotted against the Israelites, until their spy reported that Israel was strapped and ready for any attack they might bring. So Sanballat and Tobiah agreed to focus on taking down Nehemiah instead. Nehemiah was not falling for the many traps that were set against him. Even when his people became fearful and weary, he was able to encourage the Israelites, and they carried on, having "...a mind to work" (Nehemiah 4: 6b).

In life, even as a Born Again, Blood-Bought Believer, we may falter like the children of Israel and wind up in God's permissive will instead of His perfect will. This can often lead to challenges, causing us to feel scattered, empty and lying in ruin, much like Jerusalem was before Nehemiah and Erza came on the scene to rebuild it. For some of us, the work in our proverbial "building" either was once standing according to it's original design, but after setbacks and discouragement, began falling apart; or our building never was quite "built up" the way the original design was intended for it to be.

In simple terms, some of us might have started out on this Christian walk, steadily growing, stirring up our spiritual gifts and doing what we were called to do, before encountering roadblocks that have shaken our foundations. While others of us may have a sincere desire to grow in their relationship with God and be used by God, however disappointments and feelings of inadequacy and dejection have been a constant hindrance to walking in the fruition of God's plan and purpose for our lives. Whichever of these aforementioned scenarios applies to you, be not dismayed, Child of God. I have written this book to help bring hope, healing, and encouragement to YOU!

As you read through these pages and learn a little bit about my life and testimony, I pray that you will receive renewed strength and joy. Beloved, please know that even though you have been "troubled on every side, [you are] not distressed; [you might be] perplexed, but [you are] not in despair; persecuted, but not forsaken; cast down, but [definitely] not destroyed" (2 Corinthians 4: 8-9 KJV). I love how The Message Bible presents this passage between verses seven through twelve:

If you only look at *us*, you might well miss the brightness. We carry this precious Message around in the unadorned clay pots of our ordinary lives…We've been surrounded and battered by troubles, but we're not demoralized; we're not sure what to do, but we know that God knows what to do; we've been spiritually terrorized, but God hasn't left our side; we've been thrown down, but we haven't broken. What they did to Jesus, they do to us—trial and torture, mockery and murder; what Jesus did among them, he does in us—He lives! Our lives are at constant risk for Jesus' sake, which makes Jesus' life all the more evident in us. While we're going through the worst, you're getting in on the best!

So Beloved, no matter where you are in your Christian walk, please be of good cheer (John 16: 33)! Don't stop building yourself up in your most holy faith (Jude 1: 20-21). Believe that "He who has begun a good work in you is able to complete it" (Philippians 1: 6)! Go with me on this journey as you prepare to experience abundant living and enter into the FRUITION[1] of God's plan and purpose[2] for your life!

---

[1] Fruition: attainment of anything desired; realization; accomplishment: enjoyment, as of something attained or realized; state of bearing fruit ("Fruition Definition & Meaning | Dictionary.com," 2021).

[2] Purpose: all of your experiences, talents, relationships, and everything else that you are, which exists for a reason that God combined with all of the uniqueness inside of you to serve Him in specific ways that nobody else can (Rowley, 2022).

CHAPTER ONE

Birth Order

Do you ever hear jokes told about how people's actions and behaviors in response to certain situations are a direct result of where their place is that they fall in family dynamics? Some people grew up as an only child. Others might be the oldest or youngest sibling, while some people fall somewhere in the middle. Somewhat statistically, but more so stereotypically speaking (because of course this isn't the case for everyone), the oldest child tends to be the more responsible, mature one in the family, who has set the standard and blazed the trail for their siblings coming up after them. The middle child(ren) can often be more carefree, while whimsically vying for their parents' attention. The youngest child seemingly can do nothing wrong, is spoiled and adored by all. Yet an only child is looked upon as being creative, but selfish because they never really had to be in a constant state of occupying the same space and sharing things with other children for extended periods of time, unlike those who have grown up with siblings.

If you take a minute to reflect on where your place has been in the birth order of your family, does any of this sound familiar? According to psychotherapist Alfred Adler's' early 1900's Birth Order Theory, children's personalities and behaviors are reflected by the environment that they live in and family dynamics (ranging from only child to oldest, youngest and everything in between), and not their own inherent qualities. The Adlerian theory argues that whether a child was physically born in a certain order in their families, or whether they have assumed the role of that which is outside of their own natural order, due to family needs, etc, determines their behavior and personality traits.

Although many would argue that their role within their own family dynamics was atypical of the qualities that their birth order is presumed to be, they still have found that their place in their household was reflective of their parent(s) or guardian(s) and other children they grew up with, if any. Yet and still, even if individuals had a pleasant childhood experience, or came to terms with the roles and responsibilities that they assumed in their homes, oftentimes some may feel that, despite any accomplishments or recognitions they received and despite their own level of usefulness and efficiency around the house and overall positive behavior, they may still feel a level of regret, guilt and neglect. Overall, I had a very positive and pleasant upbringing as the youngest child. Nevertheless, my natural birth order disposition, often caused feelings of negativity towards myself; and to this day, still causes me to reflect deeply and internalize who I am and how my personality has both positively and negatively influenced raising my own children.

As the youngest child, I was perceived to be the spoiled one, that *never* seemed to get in trouble or needed to be disciplined, causing my siblings, I'm sure, some level of resentment growing up. Nevertheless, as the youngest, and in my own spontaneously whimsical, and impulsive way, I was not as devoted to my education, as my siblings were (nor as my parents had been when they were growing up). I was also not as athletic and barely scratched the surface in being recognized for academic or athletic achievement.

My siblings all received Urban League Black Scholars awards in high school. An empty space lingered on the wall until I graduated high school without that recognition, which was eventually replaced by my eldest sibling's "Who's Who Among African American College Students" plaque. Sure, I got a couple trophies a time or two for my participation in cheerleading, and singing in chorus, but, I deemed it nothing in comparison to my siblings' many trophies and accomplishments. My sister had beauty pageant trophies, soccer and cheerleading awards, and my brothers received *many* trophies and plaques for their athleticism and ability to break school records in track and field and football.

But not only was I not as athletic or scholarly, I was also silently struggling with who I was as a person and the fact that I was always a plus sized kid, who was not all that popular and took any form of criticism to heart, when made fun of for my appearance or lack of scholastic aptitude. Nevertheless, from the outside looking in, I was seen as confident, outspoken, a natural born leader, authoritative and even intimidating to some people.

In the midst of my internal turmoil with myself and wanting to be liked, accomplished and recognized, I was also a church kid. I was truly a *churchy* church kid by the time I was in high school. Though I had many imperfections and did not always make the best choices, one thing was more than certain, I was in love with the Lord Jesus Christ and I was committed to serving Him and growing in my relationship with Him, in which case, I was called in the ministry when I was a freshman in high school. I was taught by my Pastor and began preaching and teaching the gospel at that time. Through the ups and downs of my middle and high school experience and beyond, I ultimately had to embrace the renowned words to a familiar hymn that was easy for me to believe about others, but not for myself. Truly, "there is room at the cross for you." Yes, "There [really] is room at the cross for you. Though millions, yes they have come, there is room just for one. At the cross, there is room just for you ([*ME*])." Accepting this truth was a process that I will continue discussing throughout this book.

CHAPTER TWO

Insignificant significance

During my adolescent years, I experienced popularity limitations, most likely because not only was I the plus sized kid, but more so because I was that obnoxiously rigid church girl who inadvertently ultimately drove everyone away from me who was actually trying to be my friend. However, when I was in church, I felt renewed strength. I felt like I had a place where I belonged and where I was loved; and that was really all that mattered to me. Even though most of the other kids my age at church ended up resenting me (for either taking on solos that used to be theirs in choir, excelling in Sunday School, being called upon for various tasks, and for being deemed a positive role model and example for them to follow), I did not care because I had the love and acceptance of my senior pastor and his wife, the co-pastor, whom were like second parents to me.

Throughout high school, growing up in a small church, I received a great deal of care and nurture from my leaders, being a youngster who was on fire for Christ and had a genuine desire to live for Him and serve Him. For me, any negative experiences of being an outcast at school was grossly outweighed by the sense of belonging and nurture that I received at church. So much so, that I longed to be at church *all* of the time. I looked forward to Bible Study, Friday Night Services, Choir and Praise and Worship Team rehearsals, revivals, conferences, Sunday School, Vacation Bible School, you name it! My passion for God and ministry drove me to pursue an education in theological studies from one of the nation's leading Christian institutions, Oral Roberts University, in Tulsa, Oklahoma.

While a student at ORU, I had some amazing experiences in my Christian walk. But it was there that my eyes were opened to the proverbial dark side of ministry and the multifaceted ways that the *church* (in general) can be messy. Experiencing this greatly disheartened me and made me feel a certain level of apathy toward the church. Nevertheless, I was eager to graduate and get back home to my church where I grew up, be welcomed back with open arms, and serve in ministry.

However, upon returning home, things panned out *much* differently than I had anticipated. Although I *was*, in fact, received with open arms *initially*, things were *very* different. In the six years that I was back home serving in the ministry I grew up in before I eventually moved to California in pursuit of my doctorate, I was miserable. Things had seemingly gone from bad to worse in a short span of time, and I felt so overwhelmingly insignificant and unwanted. The first year that I was in California was a tremendous time of growth and healing. At that point, during my time of healing and the Holy Spirit ministering to me, I came to understand why I had felt so miserable for the six years prior to moving.

Well, remember that birth order phenomenon I discussed earlier? As it turns out, there was some merit to that Adlerian theory after all...*especially* in ministry. Up to that point of graduating with my Bachelor of Theology in Pastoral Christian Ministries with an emphasis in Evangelism from ORU, all I had ever known, was being the spoiled baby of my natural family (where I was well-taken care of, loved and nurtured) and then practically the "only child," so to speak, ministerially, throughout high school. There had been so much love and attention on me during those times, that I had not even realized that I had shifted into being the "eldest sibling," without recognizing things for what they were. When I moved back home from ORU, I now had *several* "younger siblings" in the ministry, where they were all learning and growing spiritually. Not all of them were naturally younger than me in age, but younger in the sense of beginning their ministerial training *well* after I began mine many years prior.

During this season, many things transpired in ministry. With so much going on around me, from evolving personalities to meeting ministerial mandates and expectations, to getting accustomed to various relational dynamics, I allowed myself to feel resentment and bitterness toward ministry. In the midst of my hurt and heartache, I sought solace, refuge and relief by becoming very promiscuous. I had reached a breaking point and decided that the proverbial eagle had been stirring her nest[3] long enough. I was ready to fly out on my own and leave that source of pain behind me. Not realizing at the time that I was needing to experience growth

---

[3] Deuteronomy 32:11-12a-"As an eagle stirs up its nest, Hovers over its young, Spreading out its wings, taking them up, Carrying them on its wings, So the LORD alone led him..." (NKJV).

in certain areas of my life that would help me to receive emotional healing and mental wellness, while enabling me to develop coping skills with the things that I had no control over that surrounded me; I had to learn that the needs of the ministry were different now. However, I often felt like the "odd man out," and isolated during this time, which adversely affected my feelings of myself.

I had already gotten my Master's degree in Education and had begun my teaching career a year and a half after I moved back home from undergrad. So, I wanted to just get away, start fresh and pursue a doctoral degree in Educational Leadership from Azusa Pacific University in Azusa, California. Even though I was moving out of hurt, under the guise of postgraduate studies, God had other plans. He ordered my steps and confirmed that I was meant to move out there for a season, where, as I mentioned earlier, I received the greatest "balm in Gilead" and truly began to heal from all of my hurts.

Ultimately, during those six years that I was back home in Rochester, in between moving from Tulsa and moving to Los Angeles, I encountered a lot of ministerial challenges that I allowed to frustrate and discourage me. But in the process of healing and growth while living in California, I began rediscovering my worth and value as a woman of God in this world. Though I was once downtrodden and felt like an insignificant outcast, God healed and delivered me, and He resealed my place of significance in His sight and in His Kingdom. In the next chapter, I will discuss how I came to embrace what God says about me.

CHAPTER THREE

God Sees Me

Sometimes, we experience such great disappointment and devastation in our lives that we can lose sight of who we are and who God says that we are. Thoughts of rejection and despondency overtake us when we fail to recognize or believe the truth of God's Word and His heart toward us. In times of weakness and in our darkest hours, it can be tempting to give up and walk away, whether from the Faith or from life itself, but there is always a glimmer of hope. Light shines in darkness as a reminder that we can always find our way back to the place where we belong. When we are lost in a rough storm at sea, Jesus is the lighthouse that illuminates our path and makes the way clear for us. He is our peace and shelter in the midst of a storm; and He is truly a very present help in the time of trouble (John 8:12; Isaiah 4:6; Psalm 46:1).

When God told Abraham that he would be the father of many nations and make his name great, he and his wife Sarah leaned to their own understanding, antithetical to Proverbs

3: 5[4]. Sarah was barren and did not see any way in the world that God would give them a son. So she told her husband, Abraham, to procreate with her maidservant, Hagar[5]. Upon conceiving Ishmael, Hagar began to despise her mistress, Sarah, who in turn began to mistreat Hagar. As a result, Hagar fled from Sarah and Abraham. On her journey, an angel of the Lord spoke to Hagar at a wellspring between Kadesh and Bered and told her to go back to Sarah and continue to serve and submit to her. Doing so would also increase her descendants. Hagar proclaimed that the place she received a word from God was Beer Lahai Roi, which means "the well of the Living One Who sees me" (Genesis 16: 1-16).

Beloved, even through navigating the trickiest of life's vicissitudes, we must remember that God knows all, sees all and He truly *does* SEE us. When I was struggling to realize and understand the love of Christ and the magnitude of His love for me, I was clouded by all of the negativity that I had experienced and had allowed Satan's voice to overshadow

---

[4] Proverbs 3: 5-"Trust in the Lord with all thine heart and lean not to thine own understanding."
[5] Note that Sarah and Abraham were *technically* still called Sarai and Abram during this time period, prior to them having Isaac.

that which I already knew concerning my life. Sure, I was still actively serving in ministry, and it was extremely easy to believe in Christ's love for His people when it came to others. However, for me, I felt that I always came in second place to being a recipient of His love, in comparison to His love for everyone else in the world.

What is it that you have been struggling with that has been keeping you from fully embracing the love of Christ in your life? Have you become so jaded that you find it challenging to engage in the worship experience during church services? Let us always remember the power and benefits of praise and worship. When you praise and worship the Lord, you are allowing the Holy Spirit to do a mighty work inside of you. Praise enables you to shed off carnal and fleshly thoughts as you thank God for all that He has done for you, and all that He has brought you through. Then, when you worship God for who He *is*, you are postured to receive from the Lord and allow His Spirit to come upon you. This is a time when the burden-removing, yoke-destroying power of God is made manifest in the worship experience. As you stand before the very presence of God, in the Most Holy Place[6], it is there that you experience Christ's love for us and understand the weight of His glory, knowing that He loves you enough to have died just for you.

Undoubtedly, Hagar was faced with many different emotions as she left the home of her mistress, Sarah. There she was, minding her own business, doing her job, and then was asked to have sexual relations with the man of the house and carry his baby. Likely, Hagar never thought of Abraham in that way before, but wanted to be an obedient servant. After everything was said and done, through a process of being now soul-tied to her boss's husband, experiencing pregnancy hormonal changes, and feeling like her boss was low-key resenting her, Hagar felt confident in her ability to do something her boss could *not* do: conceive a child. Yet

---

[6] The Holy of Holies refers to the back, inner room of Moses' tabernacle and the temples that took the tabernacle's place, starting with Solomon's Temple. The Holy of Holies was a perfect cube and contained the Ark of the Covenant. The terms "Most Holy Place" and "Holy of Holies" are interchangeable, depending on the version of the Bible one uses. The Holy of Holies served as a representation of God's presence with the nation of Israel. The veil protected the sinful people of Israel from God's holiness. The death of Jesus upon the cross ended the need for this method of worship, opening access to God for all who would believe in Jesus as God's Son (*What Was the "Most Holy Place" or the "Holy of Holies"?*, n.d.).

Hagar was confused by the shift in dynamics occurring all around her. When Sarah began dealing with her harshly, Hagar was fed up and did not want to have to deal with her anymore. She must have also felt kicked to the curb and rejected after she gave of her womb to help out her mistress, which was odd because she was only trying to be obedient to Sarah and helpful to her in the first place.

So, as Hagar set out on her journey, emotional and dejected, a visitation from a heavenly host was probably the last thing she expected to occur. When she was told to go back to where she came from and continue serving Sarah, Hagar could have felt surprised that God would even take the time to send a message to *her*. Nevertheless, she quickly realized that, in fact, she *did* have value and importance in the sight of God, and therefore honored and recognized the Lord, calling Him, "the God who sees *Me*."

Beloved, GOD SEES YOU ! ! ! ! ! Scripture tells us that God keeps track of all of our sorrows, and He collects our tears in a bottle, recording each one in His book (Psalm 56:8). God sees you when you feel broken and discouraged. God sees you when you are lonely and afraid. God sees you when you are in a storm. God sees you whether peace is still, or chaos and turmoil are surrounding you. He sees you on the mountaintop and He sees you in the valley. God sees you in spite of your flaws and He sees the good in you, even when you can't see the good in yourself. And God sees your heart when you do your best, give of yourself selflessly, even when those around you do not see you, misunderstand your motives or lack appreciation for you.

Meditate upon the Word of God and speak the following scriptures over your life:

> "The LORD your God is in your midst, A Warrior who saves. He will rejoice over you with joy; He will be quiet in His love [making no mention of your past sins], He will rejoice over you with shouts of joy" (Zephaniah 3: 17 AMP).

> "But thou, O LORD, art a shield for me; my glory, and the lifter up of mine head" (Psalm 3: 3 KJV).

"'For the mountains may move and the hills disappear, but even then my faithful love for you will remain. My covenant of blessing will never be broken,' says the LORD, who has mercy on you" (Isaiah 54: 10 NLT).

"But God showed His love to us. While we were still sinners, Christ died for us" (Romans 5: 8 NLV).

"So that Christ may dwell in your hearts through your faith. And may you, having been [deeply] rooted and [securely] grounded in love, be fully capable of comprehending with all the saints (God's people) the width and length and height and depth of His love [fully experiencing that amazing, endless love]; and [that you may come] to know [practically, through personal experience] the love of Christ which far surpasses [mere] knowledge [without experience], that you may be filled up [throughout your being] to all the fullness of God [so that you may have the richest experience of God's presence in your lives, completely filled and flooded with God Himself]" (Ephesians 3: 17-19 AMP).

These are just a few of the many scriptures in the Word of God that speak to the love of God and Christ's love for us. As you read these words, insert *your* name in there and make it personal. Post these verses and others around your house, write them on your bathroom mirror with dry erase markers, or even eyeliner or lipstick, if you have to! The more you speak and declare the Word of God over yourself, the more it becomes a part of you, the more you receive it, and the more you *truly experience* the love of Christ. He sees you; He knows you and He loves you!

CHAPTER FOUR

Shattered Dreams, Renewed Vision

Ever since I was a little girl, there were two subject areas that fascinated me and that I excelled in. I attended Catholic schools from preschool through twelfth grade. So my religion classes were always of great interest to me. Although I was brought up in the church, my family was never Roman Catholic. So, there were many differences with our protestant beliefs in comparison with that which we learned and saw from day to day in Catholic school. Nevertheless, there were many similarities and truths taught to us that helped to lay a solid foundation in my Christian beliefs.

Learning about Jesus was a wonderful experience and it caused me to become eager to learn more about the Gospel message of salvation. At home, my parents did a great job of explaining to me why some things were not a part of our beliefs, such as praying to patron saints, or praying to Mary and acknowledging her as the co-redeemer of the world. In addition, participating in church activities such as children's choir and Sunday School, as well as attending church services regularly, motivated me to keep pursuing a greater knowledge of the triune Almighty God: including His Son, Jesus Christ, and His Holy Spirit.

I also always highly admired and respected my parents' for being poised professionals with a large vocabulary and their well-spoken use of the English language. Hearing them speak conversationally to one another and to us helped pique my interest in English Language Arts. As a child, it wasn't long before I developed a passion for grammar, writing and public speaking. My dad has always been quite the wordsmith; and my mom has always so eloquently enunciated her words and would often admonish me to do likewise. So, as it turned out, theology and "the king's English" (if you will) were two subject areas that I always found interesting, was naturally good at, and I developed a real passion for.

When I was thirteen years old, I began leading praise and worship during Sunday morning and Friday night services. By the time I was fifteen years old, I began preaching the gospel as a licensed minister; and I started making guest appearances on the local Christian radio station broadcasts, which ultimately led to me being selected to co-host a weekly radio show for young people. Being that I began ministry at a young age, and had increased participation with church activities, as a high schooler, there was absolutely no other school that I wanted to attend for college than Oral Roberts University in Tulsa, Oklahoma. Even though I already had a knack for writing, during my freshman year at ORU, I was inspired by a really kind, loving and compassionate English professor, who had tremendous grammatical, formatting and writing knowledge. For me, being in a Christian institution, studying English, writing papers from a biblical lens, and having a Godly professor really was the best of both worlds!

I had a sincere desire to grow stronger in my relationship with the Lord, and I was determined to be as involved as I could in ministry. However, seeing the carnality among many of my college peers and witnessing the heretical shift and folding of the renowned ministry I attended and completed my ministry practicum in, were tough experiences to endure. So, not long after my first year in undergrad did, I grow increasingly homesick, and appalled by the unsavory actions of many Christian peers and leaders alike. Dropping out of school was not an option for me, per my parents, so I did my absolute best to graduate early in order to move back home sooner. Needless to say, taking 23.5 college credit hours in one semester absolutely burned me out. I ended up failing courses for becoming so overwhelmed that I tried to take shortcuts, but that got me into academic trouble. I had to repeat a few classes. Nevertheless, after 3 years in undergrad, I came back home, and finished my last semester through an online studies program. I was hoping to finish at least a whole year early, but I still graduated a half year early, which gave me a huge sense of relief.

As I discussed in the previous chapters, there was a lot of woundedness and brokenness that I experienced in between those six years I was back home transitioning from undergrad to grad school, heading into my post graduate career. Aspirations and goals that I had for my life by certain points in my twenties did not pan out. Expectations and dreams for my more immediate future were never actualized, which continued to draw me deeper into despair. I wanted to be married, preaching and teaching all over the world in full-time ministry, writing books, and thriving financially. Instead, there were ministry and life lessons that I needed to learn, challenges I had yet to overcome, and adversities I had yet to conquer.

Though many dreams seemed crushed and shattered, I experienced renewed hope and vision as I began to embark upon a new endeavor. For the first time in my life, I was actually moving out on my own. No longer at home with my Mommy and Daddy, nor in a strict dormitory with curfews and other restrictions, but for the first time in my life, at age 27, I felt *officially* grown when I moved to California and lived on my own. Although I was broken and wounded, I knew without any uncertainty or hesitation that God had called me there for that season.

Upon settling into my two bedroom, one and a half bathroom, two story apartment in Westchester, California, practically *everything* fell right into place. God truly ordered my steps and led me to the right places, and the right people came into my life. He opened doors of opportunity for me as well. Psalm 30 was truly my song of praise and adoration to God. I read this daily:

"I give you all the credit, GOD—you got me out of that mess, you didn't let my foes gloat. GOD, my God, I yelled for help, and you put me together. GOD, you pulled me out of the grave, gave me another chance at life when I was down-and-out. All you saints! Sing your hearts out to GOD! Thank Him to his face! He gets angry once in a while, but across a lifetime there is only love. The nights of crying your eyes out give way to days of laughter. When things were going great, I crowed, "I've got it made. I'm GOD's favorite. He made me king of the mountain." Then you looked the other way and I fell to pieces. I called out to you, GOD; I laid my case before you "Can you sell me for a profit when I'm dead? Auction me off at a cemetery yard sale? When I'm 'dust to dust' my songs and stories of you won't sell. So listen! and be kind! Help me out of this!" You did it: you changed wild lament into whirling dance; You ripped off my black mourning band and decked me with wildflowers. I'm about to burst with song; I can't keep quiet about you. GOD, my God, I can't thank you enough" (Psalm 30: 1-12 MSG).

My hopes and dreams had been renewed and I was soon to encounter one of the biggest periods of spiritual, personal, intellectual and professional growth in my life. During which case, things were about to take an unexpected turn in the process. In the next chapter you will learn more about these experiences and how I became triumphant. The victories that I experienced were just the beginning of the fruition of purpose that I would walk in.

CHAPTER FIVE

Rejecting Rejection

The first year that I was living on my own, nearly 3,000 miles away from home, so much happened in such a short period of time. Great things were happening all around me and within me, but it wasn't completely a flowery bed of ease either. I experienced significant growing pains during my "Isle of Patmos" experience, as I called it. Although I knew that I was being led by the Holy Spirit to move to Los Angeles, the circumstances by which I was *really* moving there, were rather, much less than optimal. Similar to the Apostle John ("The Revelator"), I felt seemingly exiled to a faraway place as a result of *who* I was as a minister of the gospel. John was rejected and banished by his lonesome to an island on the west coast of Asia Minor in the Aegean Sea for preaching the message of Jesus Christ and Salvation.

Technically, I was *not* banished, per se. However, I was more so in a proverbial "eagle stirring her nest[7]" type of

---

[7] "Frustration, hunger, and discomfort are [the eaglet's] parents' intention. The parents wisely know that without this disruptive

situation as I mentioned earlier. Like Joseph told his brothers at the pinnacle of his governing career in Egypt, my sentiments were similar to his, in that, although they "intended to harm me...God intended it all for good" (Genesis 50: 20b NLT).

Leaving on my own volition was a two-fold cause. Like Abraham, by faith, I was called to venture to a new land un*known* to me, so that God could guide me to everywhere I needed to be [literally and figuratively] (Hebrews 11: 8). Likewise, I had grown tired of the constant spirit of rejection and dejection that I was feeling as a result of the many things that were changing and shifting in ministry back home. At the time of my departure, the atmosphere felt very hostile and tumultuous. Out of the various advisement sessions that I had with my senior pastor, who observed many of the things I was experiencing, he confirmed my suspicions that contention and strife was occurring because people

---

environment their young will not grow, learn, and develop the essential skills for survival. Though the eaglet does not understand this at the time, the lack of food and removal of comfort is an act of tender care and love, a gift of provision by her parents who know that without the ability to fly, she cannot survive and thrive. Unbeknownst to the eaglet, the parents are giving her the gift of flight . . . the gift of life. Faith for the Christian is like flight for an eagle: essential to survive and thrive" (Kruger, 2017).

ultimately were dealing with their own displaced insecurities and personal issues. Nevertheless, his genuine compassion towards me, spiritual guidance, encouragement, reassurance, and also his admonishing instruction to my ministerial cohort and I had truly helped me through those difficult times. This senior pastor and bishop in the Lord's house, remained fair, unbiased, and loving while I experienced these growing pains at home, and out of state, and even upon my return home for the second time. I am grateful for the Christ-like compassion and shepherding that he continuously demonstrated toward me. Without his love and guidance, I might not ever have made it, and my Christian walk could possibly look very different or even be non-existent today.

So, even though I was excited for this next chapter of my life, when I arrived at "Patmos" (Los Angeles, CA), I was fragmented. I was disheartened and I felt defeated. I was at a very critical paradox in my life. The past six years that I was on the verge of leaving behind was *the* **defining**

moment[8] of my life that altered the trajectory[9] of everything in my world. At that particular point of my life, I could have *very* easily given up, gone buck-wild, forsook God, and lived a life driven by worldliness. But instead, I remembered the words of the Apostle Paul, saying to myself repeatedly:

> Since God has so generously let [me] in on what He is doing, [I'm] not about to throw up [my] hands and walk off the job just because [I] run into occasional hard times. [I] refuse to wear masks and play games. [I] don't maneuver and manipulate behind the scenes. And [I] don't twist God's Word to suit [myself]. Rather, [I] keep everything [I] do and say out in the open, the whole truth on display, so that those who want to can see and judge for themselves in the presence of God. [I've] been surrounded and battered by troubles, but [I'm] not demoralized; [I'm] not

[8] "A *defining moment* is a point in your life when you're urged to make a pivotal decision, or when you experience something that fundamentally changes you. Not only do these moments define us, but they have a transformative effect on our perceptions and behaviors" (Council, 2017).

[9] Trajectory in the Christian sense means the progression or path followed to obtain God's will for one's life.

sure what to do, but [I] know that God knows what to do; [I've] been spiritually terrorized, but God hasn't left [my] side; [I've] been thrown down, but [I] haven't broken. What they did to Jesus, they do to [me]—trial and torture, mockery and murder; what Jesus did among them, He does in [me]—He lives! So [I'm] not giving up. How could [I]? Even though on the outside it often looks like things are falling apart on [me], on the inside, where God is making new life, not a day goes by without His unfolding grace. These hard times are small potatoes compared to the coming good times; the lavish celebration prepared for [me]. There's far more here than meets the eye. The things [I] see now are here today, gone tomorrow. But the things [I] can't see now will last forever (2 Corinthians 4: 1-2, 8-11, 16-18 MSG).

Moreover, I was being postured to embark upon some of the greatest moments of my life. Almost immediately, God led me directly to a new church home, and it was there that I met a dear sister in Christ, who was extremely instrumental in helping me get acclimated to a new state, new church home, and introduced me to many other sisters and brothers in Christ. She took me under her wing and was a true Godsend…an amazing person to know, whom I am so glad entered my life!

Before long, I became a leader in my church's young adults ministry, having had opportunities to minister through teaching, leading praise and worship and serving the people of God. This was also a season of becoming realigned with my purpose and removing all hindrances and distractions in my life. During this time, I still had a few male acquaintances "in my back pocket" in my hometown, and my new home state. But again, God caused those relationships to be completely severed, which allowed me absolutely *NO* other choice, but to press in, be pruned, be fed spiritually, nourish myself spiritually, and grow. I sat under the ministry teachings of a very renown bishop, who was the senior pastor of a mega ministry. I learned a *huge* wealth of scriptural knowledge from him, and I am so grateful to have once served in his ministry.

One day, as I sat alone, quietly in prayer at home, God revealed to me that I had been wrestling with the spirit of rejection and He was going to deliver me and set me free from it. According to Phyillis Tarbox, the spirit of rejection "victimizes its prey by causing them to feel worthless and unwanted. It employs a spirit of self-pity as its right-hand man to drive people away and allow abandonment and isolation to move in. A spirit of rejection taunts with one failure after another in hopes you will say, 'I give up!'" (Tarbox, 2015). Sometimes, people take situations as a form of rejection, even though they never were rejected to begin with. As I mentioned in chapter two, there were various changes that were occurring all around me at my home church. I experienced unknown unrequited love, awkward discomfort in navigating my way through understanding my position within my ministerial family and venturing into a new phase of my life as a saved young adult, all while trying to work out my own salvation with fear and trembling (Philippians 2: 12)! Yet at the time, I took each of these situations as a form of rejection, which became a downward spiral. God therefore showed me that I must not take on that rejection spirit, but I must rather *reject* that spirit myself.

In a still small voice, God gave me a word concerning rejection. He said I must **R**ealize **E**very **J**ourney's **E**xperience **C**reates **T**he **I**mportant **O**pportunity for **N**ewness. In the midst of hard times, devastation, desolation and dry seasons, God works things together for our good (Romans 8: 28) and creates new experiences in our lives. The following scriptures detail how we encounter newness:

> For I am about to do something new. See, I have already begun! Do you not see it? I will make a pathway through the wilderness. I will create rivers in the dry wasteland (Isaiah 43: 19 NLT).

> It is because of the Lord's loving-kindness that we are not destroyed for His loving-pity never ends. It is new every morning. He is so very faithful (Lamentations 3: 22-23 NLV).

> For I consider that the sufferings of this present time are not worthy *to be compared* with the glory which shall be revealed in us. For the earnest expectation of the creation

eagerly waits for the revealing of the sons of God. For the creation was subjected to futility, not willingly, but because of Him who subjected *it* in hope; because the creation itself also will be delivered from the bondage of [a]corruption into the glorious liberty of the children of God (Romans 8: 18-21 NKJV).

Throughout life, we experience "no's," failures and mishaps, but those things do not characterize us, nor diminish who we are as a whole…who we are in *Christ*. There will be times in our lives when we do *not* get what we want because there was something that God was keeping us from that wasn't good for us; and there will be times in our lives when the Lord will give us the desires of our hearts, but we must first wait. Let me clarify though, in terms of future spouses. I am not saying that the person someone may have initially wanted to marry is bad or that something would have gone horribly wrong if they had married them. This is not necessarily the case for anyone in a predicament such as this.

It may very well be that that particular person just was not *meant* for that individual, and that's ok!

Scripture admonishes us that if we wait on the Lord, He will give us the desires of our hearts. For the theologians reading, the verse may initially appear that I inadvertently combined Isaiah 40: 31 with Psalm 37: 4. However, as I stated, very intentionally, we must *wait* on the Lord. The Expanded Bible translation of Psalm 37: 4 says that we must "*enjoy serving* the LORD, and He will give you what you want [the requests of your heart]. Instead of "enjoy serving," other translations say to "*delight ourselves* in the Lord." This does not merely mean that we should receive joy within us, but it also means that, like a waiter in a restaurant, we must truly *serve* God. Isaiah 40:31 states that those who "*wait*" on the Lord will receive renewed strength. Though many preachers would argue the etymological derivative of this word means the same as the 'a' clause of Psalm 37:4 that I just discussed. Yet and still, the fact remains that if we delightfully focus on Christ and serve Him, we are strengthened and receive the desire of our heart (that of course, must be in alignment with the will of God for our lives and with His Word). Moreover, the experiences that we have throughout our journey, is an opportunity for us to serve God as He uses that to open doors of opportunity for new beginnings in our life.

By proclaiming the Word of God over my life and acknowledging that God was preparing me for the greater, yet to be seen, I broke free from the bondage of the spirit of rejection. God gave me a confession to declare over myself daily, and that is what I did (See Appendix A). I typed it out, put it on my wall, and had a time of prayer, praise, worship, confession, listening to His voice and healing. I encourage you as well to use this confession to declare over yourself daily. Or you may also be led to write down your own in the notes section toward the back of the book. I also listened to Fred Hammond's 2009 album, *Love Unstoppable*, which was very instrumental in helping me become set free and grow spiritually during this time frame in my life. In particular, "Best Thing That Ever Happened" was a powerful tool of worship as I allowed the Holy Spirit to minister to me. See Appendix B for the lyrics.

CHAPTER SIX

Beloved of God

Remember when you were in school, and you had a huge test coming up, but instead of studying, you procrastinated in some of the most useless ways imaginable? Maybe you chose to hang out with friends, or just chill by yourself watching movies, or shopping, or even napping. One thing is for certain, despite the level of procrastination that you engaged in, you *probably* never really actually got around to studying…at least not to the magnitude that you should have in order to ace the test with ease. What was the end result of your procrastination? Undoubtedly, it was failing the test. *Sometimes* there were opportunities to raise your test score, by either making test corrections (ie. computations on a math exam), retaking the test, or in some cases, repeating the course or the grade level. If that has ever happened to you (perhaps more than once for some of us), one thing is for certain. Eventually, you grew tired of having to repeat the same course content and taking the same test over and over, So, you finally buckled down, studied, and worked hard to apply yourself so that you could pass.

In one way or another, this analogy was similar to what I experienced in relationships. After I had moved back home from undergrad and after I got my Master's degree when I was around 24 years old, and prior to moving to California, that was my time of experimenting and indulging in relationships with various men. No matter how much I knew that they were wrong for me, and in many ways bad for me, I *still* continued to be in relationships and/or have relations with them. After I had moved to California, there was about one more guy that I met and had a very short-lived pseudo relationship with, but God said enough was *enough*! As I had mentioned in the last chapter, God intervened and caused all of my male acquaintances, associates and relationships to vaporize. God got me alone, so that I really had *no* other choice, than to seek Him and grow in my walk with Him.

The pruning, the healing, the deliverance and the restoration began taking place at that time. By February of 2010, I was absolutely completely and *totally* focused on my relationship with Jesus. I had the most amazing worship, personal devotional and Bible study sessions by myself, and I heard the voice of God daily, ever so clearly. I was fully in love with Jesus Christ and I was not going to let *anyone* deter me from that love, nor cause me to lose focus in that season. But one night, in Bible Study at church, I met a man, whom I honestly thought could have been the brother of the last guy that I had dated. After class, I went to him and asked him if he had a brother by the name of that guy (because I was really about to tell him that he needed to check his brother, who was a total jerk, etc)... But, as it turned out, this man was an only child. This gentleman was actually very kind, genuine and unlike any man I had ever met before. He very politely and respectfully walked me across the street, and walked me to my car in the parking garage. During that walk, we had such a delightful conversation that we ended up talking in the parking lot for three hours! We exchanged contact information and parted ways. When I went back to my apartment, and the next morning, I sounded the alarm. I told practically *everyone* that I knew who had been a spiritual covering over me and my family, that I had met the most amazing guy the previous night, and I wanted them to help bombard heaven with me to pray him away!

I was convinced that this was just another distraction and hindrance to my spiritual growth and maturity. Afterall, I had been doing so well and completely focused on Jesus! Much to my surprise, I kept hearing the same responses over and over again. I was encouraged not to assume this was a work of the devil coming to distract me (considering the other dudes were major distractions/hindrances), and to prayerfully consider that this may in fact be my betrothed that God sent to me. Especially since he came correct!

So, who exactly was this guy, you might ask? As it turns out, this guy *really* was my betrothed...my husband-to-be, Mr. Gregory R. Ellis II. God's timing is always perfect and in retrospect, the manner in which God presented Greg to me, and he found me, truly gave credence to the Christian cliche: once you completely surrender to God and become fully content and satisfied with *Him*, He blesses you with your spouse-to-be. Ironically, even though I was totally focused on Jesus, I knew in my spirit that God would soon prepare me to embark upon the next season of my life, marriage. I ordered a few books on Amazon (which I've listed in Appendix C), thinking that I'd keep them in my repertoire for when I really needed them. But I kid you not...

When the books arrived on March 9, 2010, I skimmed through different sections of these books, and *the very next day* was when I went to Bible Study and met my future husband.

Greg was looking for a *wife*. He was ready to settle down and find his "good thing" that God was going to bless him with (Proverbs 18:22). Come to find out, Greg had been regularly attending singles ministry Bible studies for quite some time, in efforts to spiritually strengthen and equip himself, while mentally preparing for his future wife. So, when I met Greg, he was marriage-minded and did everything in his power to show forth the "husband potential" that he possessed. Greg was extremely chivalrous, mindful of me, thoughtful, respectful, considerate, intelligent, and wise. Shortly after we began courting one another, we began our 6 months of premarital advisement. These classes were an excellent foundational resource for our relationship, as we both consistently prayed and had the desire to be at the center of God's will. Marriage followed soon after.

Throughout our courtship, engagement, and newlywed experiences, I came to grow all the more spiritually. Now, in our twelfth year of marriage, of course, we have had our share of marital woes, ups and downs. Even though I have questioned at times whether or not I made the right decision to get married to Greg, and despite the ebbs and flows, mountain high and valley low experiences, I can truly say that I have gained a greater understanding of the love of God. Being the wife of a man of God has enabled me to see that the love that my husband has for me, is an extension of God's love for me. Greg and I both have unique idiosyncrasies, that in some ways compliment one another's unique personalities, and in other ways, are polar opposites of our personalities: of which, may also be attributed to male and female dynamics in general.

Ultimately, Greg's character as a man of God, and how he has been treating me as his best friend and his wife in our marriage, has a lot to say about the love of Christ Jesus, our Lord. Since I have known Greg, in the times when we have had "intense fellowship" (arguments and disagreements), Greg absolutely has *NEVER* personally attacked me, nor has he insulted me, disrespected me, nor emotionally abused me.

If his voice has ever needed to be elevated, it has always been to interrupt any negativity, and disrespect that I may have shown towards him during an argument. Nevertheless, despite any of these times, there are two things that Greg and I always come away with from the disagreement: 1.) a continued open line of communication that we have kept, while never walking away from each other upset during the argument, and 2.) prayer. Ever since I have known Greg, no matter what, he will always take me by the hand and/or embrace me, apologize for any offense or hurt he may have caused me, and *PRAY*, no matter *how* upset I might be with him, and unwilling to let something go.

Through the years, Greg has adhered to the Word of God, stating that " Husbands, [should] love [their] wives, just as Christ also loved the church and gave Himself for it...[because] men ought to love their wives as their own bodies...[Therefore, he must] love his wife as himself, and let [his] wife see that she respects her husband" (Ephesians 5: 25, 28a, & 33 MEV). And although Greg is not perfect, nor has our entire relationship been, I can most assuredly say that Greg has truly been patient, kind, respectful and compassionate towards me. Because God is love (I John 4:

16b), if we exchange the word charity with "God" in First Corinthians 13, we can truly see how amazing God's love for us really is!

> [God] is patient and kind. [God] is not jealous or boastful or proud or rude. [He] does not demand [His] own way. [He] is not irritable, and [He] keeps no record of being wronged. [He] does not rejoice about injustice but rejoices whenever the truth wins out. [God] never gives up, never loses faith, is always hopeful, and endures through every circumstance (I Corinthians 13: 4-7).

Yes, Bible Scholars, some of these attributes are theoretically debatable from an exegetically etymological perspective, but I will not get into that because *you* know what I mean. Nevertheless, these descriptions for charity (love) exemplify how we must love one another (particularly our spouse), demonstrated through God's love for us.

Scripture encourages us to know God through love saying,

*"Beloved, let us love one another, for love is of God; and everyone who loves is born of God and knows God. He who does not love does not know God, for God is love. In this the love of God was manifested toward us, that God has sent His only begotten Son into the world, that we might live through Him. In this is love, not that we loved God, but that He loved us and sent His Son to be the propitiation for our sins. Beloved, if God so loved us, we also ought to love one anothe*r" (I John 4: 7-11 NKJV).

We can also *see* God through love. The Word goes on to declare that "*No one has seen God at any time. If we love one another, God abides in us, and His love has been perfected in us. By this we know that we abide in Him, and He in us, because He has given us of His Spirit. And we have seen and testify that the Father has sent the Son as Savior of the world. Whoever confesses that Jesus is the Son of God, God abides in him, and he in God. And we have known and believed the love that God has for us. God is love, and he who abides in love abides in God, and God in him*" (I John 4: 12-16 NKJV). We *are* the beloved of God, therefore we must "embrace, as the elect of God, holy and *beloved*, a spirit of mercy, kindness, humbleness of mind, meekness, and longsuffering" (Colossians 1: 12 MEV).

Greg was and is the blessing in my life that I didn't know that I needed. Even as Greg and I are continuously developing as individuals (spiritually, personally, intellectually, emotionally, and even financially), and we are being pruned by the Holy Spirit, God knows exactly *who* we are, *what* we are, *where* we are and *where* we are going, *when* we are going to get there, *and* how He is going to get us there. Greg's love for God, for me and for our children is just a glimpse of the mirrored intense love that God has for him and me, and our beautiful children. Though all marriage relationships go through storms, our charge is to continue loving one another and growing in our relationship as husband and wife, while cultivating our relationship with God.

CHAPTER SEVEN

Righteousness of God

About two years after Greg and I got married, we got pregnant. Sadly, that pregnancy ended in a miscarriage. Even now, not a day goes by that I don't think about my unborn baby and how much {he} would have grown by now. Nevertheless, we know that we will see {him} in Heaven one day. For me, this devastating occurrence temporarily became another reason to be down on myself. And there I went, not able to keep myself from reflecting on my birth order woes. I thought to myself that surely this happened to *me* for a reason. Afterall, I've *always* been the one that something unfortunate has happened to and not them (like having to wear braces in high school); and none of my older siblings in their marriages at the time had dealt with an arduous loss of that nature before. So, I reasoned that surely, God must have been punishing me for *something*. Perhaps it was because of all of my debauchery in my twenties. Or maybe it could have been because of my unintentionally overly confident, and candidly rigid self, which was off-putting to a lot of people in high school and college.

There I was, in shock and believing the lies the adversary was feeding me. These lies were similar to the lies that Job's friends brought to him, accusing Job of having been sinful and at fault, considering all of the turmoil and tribulation he was going through (Job 4-23). But then, just like that, I was reminded about Jesus's words in response to His disciples questioning Him about who was sinful (at fault) in the blind man's life because he was visually impaired. Jesus told the disciples that the man's blindness had nothing to do with his nor his parents' sinful (Adamic[10]) nature. But he was blind so that "the works of God [would] be made manifest in him" (John 9: 3b). So, I realized that, in God's sovereignty, despite my grief, His handiwork would continue to be made manifest or *displayed* and *illustrated* (as the Amplified Version describes it) in my life. No matter what, God will always get the glory in my life. Even when we, as the believing body of Christ, might feel unrighteous, unworthy, and wretched, we can rest assured that "God made Him who knew no sin [(Jesus)] to be sin for

---

[10] Adamic Nature-stems from the "Original Sin" committed in the Garden of Eden. Every man, woman, and child on planet Earth is born with it (Rickroehm, 2011).

us, that we might become the *righteousness of God* in Him" (II Corinthians 5: 21 NKJV).

Fast forward about 3 years after God took our "angel baby[11]" to heaven, and after we had our beautiful "rainbow baby[12]," our son, Kristopher, we had our "miracle baby[13]," our daughter, Karrington. Her arrival into our family came with many obstacles, and thus, I needed the same reminder from the revelation I received in John 9. Karrington had a complicated medical journey, upon being born prematurely. Throughout her stay in the Neonatal Intensive Care Unit, Karrington had to endure multiple procedures, including gastrointestinal and cardiac surgeries. At the time, having a baby in the NICU and a 19-month-old at home presented various challenges. Kristopher was too young to come to the NICU and yet I had a very sick newborn, who equally

---

[11] Angel baby-used to refer to a baby who died in the womb or shortly after birth (*Oxford English Dictionary*, n.d.)

[12] Rainbow baby-A rainbow baby is a term for a baby that's born after the parents have a pregnancy loss. The name draws on the symbol of the rainbow, representing beauty after a dark time (WebMD Editorial Contributors, 2021).

[13] Miracle baby-Often born with under-developed lungs, gut, brain, ears and eyes, when they survive against all odds they are called miracle babies. With the sometimes-unexpected early arrival of these vulnerable, underdeveloped babies comes a great deal of stress and often guilt for many mothers (ABC News, 2018).

needed her Mommy and Daddy. At the time, I was recovering from a difficult, life-threatening cesarean procedure, as I had developed an infection, causing me to go into labor early. When Karrington was born and whisked away to the NICU, I saw the look of panic on the doctors' faces, as I laid on the operating table, nauseous, faint, and bleeding out. Thankfully, I survived and recovered. Nevertheless, I needed the grace and mercy of God to help me make it through this NICU baby and toddler season I was in.

I was tempted to fall into depression and blame myself once more for having a baby who was sick, with severe medical needs. But thanks be unto God, because of His lovingkindness, I was not consumed (Lamentations 3:22). The Living Bible translation of that passage declares that, "It is only the Lord's mercies that have kept [me] from complete destruction. Great is His faithfulness; His loving-kindness begins afresh each day." I came to the realization and understanding that, even though we had a difficult road ahead of us, I was truly *blessed* to be chosen by God to be Karrington's mother, and God graced us with the ability to care for and nurture her in the manner in which she needed.

I was thankful to be able to properly care for our son, while *still* being able to be with our daughter in the hospital *every single day* of those six months that she spent in the hospital. And every single night I called and spoke to the nurses on the unit who were taking care of Karrington, to get updates on how she was doing.

Even though Karrington has a genetic condition and has had some developmental delays, she is thriving. Karrington is victorious, healthy and doing well; and we decree total healing over her life. Kristopher has had his share of difficulties as well, having experienced anaphylaxis from allergic reactions and hospitalization as a result of asthma exacerbation, among other challenges. Yet, he too amazes us with his triumphant brilliance and joy of the Lord that is in his heart. As the father and mother of Kristopher and Karrington, Greg and I are honored to be their parents and we thank God daily for blessing us with them. We speak the Word of God over their lives, regularly pray over them, encourage and affirm them in who they are in Christ Jesus (See Appendix E for a sample Daily Affirmation for Kids: God gave me these words for our babies while my daughter was in the NICU and we have been saying them ever since).

What experiences have you endured that you needed God's grace and mercy to make it through? Perhaps as you are reading this book, you are in the midst of a struggle right now and you need the strength and courage to continue fighting. Beloved, know that you are not alone, nor are you forsaken or forgotten. God sees you and He will see you through. Don't give up. You are the apple of God's eyes (Zechariah 2: 8), and as scripture tells us, "[God's] grace is sufficient for you, for [His] strength is made perfect in weakness…So…take pleasure in weaknesses, in reproaches, in hardships, in persecutions, and in distresses... For when I am weak, then I am strong" (II Corinthians 12: 9-10 MEV). So beloved, don't blame yourself and feel down on yourself for the way your life is unfolding. Afterall, "even before He made the world, God loved us and chose us in Christ to be holy and without fault in His eyes" (Ephesians 1: 4 NLT). Remember, you *are* His righteousness!

CHAPTER EIGHT

Anonymity and Obscurity

Rewinding to when I moved back home from my undergraduate program at ORU, things had gradually gotten a lot different in ministry. Not only was I trying to emotionally and spiritually recover from the things I experienced down in Tulsa, but as I continued in the ministry, I felt more and more obsolete, while being more and more obscure. By definition, I was being less and less used, out of date and replaced by something new (*Oxford English Dictionary*, n.d.). Many of the relationships and rapport I had established with other pastors and leaders that my church fellowshipped with when I was in high school had significantly diminished. It seemed as though practically *nobody* remembered who I was or even cared. Even in the present day, I get a lot of "friend request rejections" and "unfriendings" on social media from church people (past and present) because they either don't remember me, or don't care to be in contact with me. But, it's all good. I certainly don't lose any sleep over it.

As Jesus was growing up and even well into His young adulthood, He was incredibly wise beyond His years, gifted and anointed. Yet, Jesus held a significant level of anonymity because He was not renowned at this time, nor had He "gone public" with His ministry. Even at the wedding feast in Cana, Jesus gave His mother push back about performing a public miracle because His "hour had not yet come" (John 2: 4). The amplified translation says that His time to act and be revealed had not yet arrived. Jesus was speaking metaphorically about ultimately fulfilling His purpose according to His divine timeline to begin His ministry publicly, and be the sacrificial Lamb of God, who saves the world from sin and death. Nevertheless, as God would have it, Jesus performed His first miracle in turning the water into wine at the wedding feast in Cana, catapulting Him into His next season of ministry.

One thing to bear in mind is that we must not grow weary while doing the work of the Lord. As I mentioned in the earlier chapters, I have always had a strong and sincere desire to serve in ministry, full-time. I know my calling, which includes some of the five-fold ministry gifts[14]. I also know the anointing that is on my life to ultimately help others. Unfortunately, though, the various experiences that I have had going to a new church (circumstantially, as a result of relocation), people have not always been as eager to receive me, nor allow me to serve to the magnitude that I have already been equipped. Understandably so, as the Bible states and pastors often proclaim, they must "know them that labor among [them] (I Thessalonians 5: 12). However, this scripture is often taken out of context. The Apostle Paul was admonishing lay people in the church, what their posture *ought* to be toward their pastors. The New Living Translation of this verse and the next says, "Dear brothers and sisters, honor those who are your leaders in the Lord's work. They work hard among you and give you spiritual guidance. Show them great respect and wholehearted love because of their work. And live peacefully with each other" (vv. 12-13). This has *always* been my posture towards the pastors and leaders that I have

---

[14] Five-fold Ministry Gifts-"And He gave some, apostles; and some, prophets; and some, evangelists; and some, pastors and teachers; For the perfecting of the saints, for the work of the ministry, for the edifying of the body of Christ (Ephesians 4: 11-12 KJV).

served under. However, people don't always receive or properly discern this demeanor. Oftentimes, entering into established ministries with zeal and a particular level of spiritual maturity, has caused me to be labeled as being overzealous, arrogant, having an ulterior motive, and/or being overbearing. I have found though, that this suspicion does not always begin with the pastors of the church, but rather, it comes from their inner leadership team, some of whom, I have learned, ultimately feel threatened and don't want their positions tampered with thus, planting a root of negativity in the senior pastors' ears.

My desire to serve in ministry full-time has always stemmed from my love of the Lord and my desire to grow stronger in my relationship with Him. Yes, because I grew up in a place where I was nurtured and under my pastors' wings, I have always longed for that same spiritual nurturing that I once readily received as a child. I enjoyed being "shepherded" and gleaning from my leaders as I closely served them in capacities such as an armor bearer, administrative assistant and elder in the Lord's house. But seasons come and go. I just wish that my passion for serving God and His people would have never been misconstrued as arrogance or wanting the spotlight. Afterall, although I *can* preach, teach, lead praise and worship, and overall stand before people with boldness; that is not actually my *preference*, per se. I always get very nervous and would rather not have to be up in front of people. I enjoy doing administrative, behind the scenes tasks, organizing, developing, and strategic planning. So it is *ONLY* by God's grace and under *HIS* anointing that I am able to stand before people and minister to them as *HE* would have me to do so.

The Bible declares that "If someone aspires to be a church leader, he desires an honorable position" (I Timothy 3: 1 NLT). But so frequently it seems that practically *nobody* in church even remembers this scripture. More often than not, you hear testimony after testimony of people *running* from God: the people who didn't want to be in church or serve in any single capacity *whatsoever*. So, many church leaders have become desensitized when it comes to a grown, obscure person, who is not a pastor's kid, who doesn't have a *major* "weary, wounded and sad, downtrodden 'running from God'" testimony. Even during my most "messed up" times of my life, and doing wrong, I *STILL* chased after God, was *quick* to repentance and wanted to get delivered and grow spiritually. Believers can do people a disservice in church when we are quick to label them as suspicious. Many church leaders have "Judases" in their inner circle, like Jesus did. He *knew* that Judas would betray Him, and shepherds are discerning. Yet, I ask, why are there *so* many pastors that are blindsided when someone in their circle falters? Where is their discernment? Why is the reservation and concern always about the one who genuinely *wants* to serve God, but yet they fail to see, discern, investigate or believe the petty, shady unjust happenings of their inner circle? Not that this is *always* the case in ministries. Nevertheless, I have observed this several times in various ministries that I have been a part of.

Ultimately, God's timing is truly perfect. He is the One ordering our steps and navigating us through life, even when we have missteps and veer off the path that can sometimes delay our entrance into the place, He would have us to be in, in order to walk in the fullness of our specific calling. Therefore beloved, let us always remember and meditate upon these words:

"But he knows where I am and what I've done. He can cross-examine me all he wants, and I'll pass the test with honors. I've followed him closely, my feet in his footprints, not once swerving from his way. I've obeyed every word he's spoken, and not just obeyed his advice—I've treasured it" (Job 23: 10-12 MSG).

"I know what I'm doing. I have it all planned out—plans to take care of you, not abandon you, plans to give you the future you hope for. When you call on me, when you come and pray to me, I'll listen. When you come looking for me, you'll find me. Yes, when you get serious about finding me and want it more than anything else, I'll make sure you won't be disappointed" (Jeremiah 29: 11-13 MSG).

"I knew you before I formed you in your mother's womb. Before you were born, I set you apart and appointed you as my prophet to the nations" (Jeremiah 1: 5 NLT).

Moreover beloved, you are not forgotten. Though it may seem that you are obscure and looked over, God has you in the hollow of His hands and has you right where He wants you. Continue praying, continue praising, continue worshiping, and continue seeking HIM. You are fulfilling His plans even now… and yes, your best *is* yet to come!

CHAPTER NINE

Prophecy

In all of my love of the English language (both writing and speaking), and my love for humanity (saved and unsaved), these things directly correlate with a spiritual (five-fold ministry) gift that God has given to me. When I was 15, I heard the voice of God speak to me in the middle of the night. God spoke to me about what He was doing in my life by calling me to specific areas of ministry, one of which is *prophecy*.

At the time, I really had absolutely *no* idea what prophecy was or what all it entailed. As soon as I got the chance, I shared with my pastor and spiritual father what God revealed to me. As I shared about God having called me to evangelism and prophesy, I was familiar with what it means to evangelize[15], but I was still very unsure about prophecy.

---

[15] Evangelism entails fulfilling the Great Commission according to the gospel writer in Matthew 28: 18-20 (NLT)-"Jesus came and told his disciples, "I have been given all authority in heaven and

As time went on entering into my adulthood up through now, I learned more about and developed in my spiritual gifts. This enabled me to understand more about myself also. As with every spiritual gift, there are certain personality traits often attributed to the individuals who possess them.

For me, operating under a prophetic anointing and walking in this spiritual gift has taught me a lot about why certain aspects of my life have always been the way that they are. If we study the prophets of the Bible, and we analyze the ministry that they did in their day, we discover that their personalities and demeanors were much so different from how the average believer prophesying is often viewed as being today.

There is nothing wrong with words of encouragement, comfort and prosperity. In fact, by definition, the role of a prophet is to be "a spokesperson for God. The prophet admonishes, warns, directs, encourages, intercedes, teaches and counsels. He brings the word of God to the people of

---

on earth. Therefore, go and make disciples of all the nations, baptizing them in the name of the Father and the Son and the Holy Spirit. Teach these new disciples to obey all the commands I have given you. And be sure of this: I am with you always, even to the end of the age."

God and calls the people to respond" (*Role of a Prophet*, n.d.). Yet, all too often, people place so much emphasis on the encouragement attribute of a prophet, that when they encounter poor reactions to their words of admonition and rebuke, the prophet can sometimes be left feeling like a desolate outcast.

In all actuality, a prophet, more often than not, gives words of warning regarding the judgment of God in response to sinfulness, if repentance does not take place. Prophets have a tendency to be very forthright and candid, which can often cause them to be disliked by their peers (family, friends, and foes alike).

Over the years, I have come to understand my unique personality traits as it pertains to holding the office of a prophet. Prophets tend to be rather quirky, sensitive, compassionate, and often socially awkward, yet an extroverted introvert[16].

---

[16] An *Extroverted Introvert* is an *Ambivert*. An ambivert is someone who has a balance of both introversion and extroversion, with the ability to lean more into one or the other depending on the context. For example, where introverts may prefer to listen while extroverts prefer to chat, an ambivert will likely have no trouble with either. They're flexible. An ambivert's propensity for introversion and extroversion can change

As with any spiritual gift, there are a few pitfalls, or vices to be mindful of. Things made *so* much sense to me about my life when I learned more about the areas that those who stand in the office of a prophet and exercise this spiritual gift must be mindful of. In general, our spiritual gifts that God has entrusted us with are designed to empower people, while encouraging servitude, fostering spiritual growth and promoting unity. Yet, there are times when having these spiritual gifts sometimes cause individuals to become spiritually prideful and misuse what God has entrusted them with. Likewise, if not being careful, spiritual gifts can also be neglected, or conversely, overly relied upon (Parker, 2023).

Even the most sanctified, spiritually mature, completely submitted to God Christians are subject to falling into error: especially when their spiritual gifts come into the forefront. Walking in the fivefold ministry office of a prophet, there are certain areas that my life has been influenced and affected by since holding this spiritual office. In general,

---

depending on individual needs in any given moment or situation (Regan & Hallett, 2022).

prophets are motivated to expose sin by applying the Word of God to every situation (See Appendix G). Prophets are God's mouthpiece who are considered alarm-sounders in the midst of compromise and sin (*What Is the Spiritual Gift of Prophecy?*, n.d.). Even in my own imperfection, I have always desired for others to be delivered and set free from sin and death. Many times, have I cried out to God in intercession for people who I knew, knew of, or didn't even know, but was led to pray for specific people in certain situations around the world.

I have had a tendency to be very "matter of fact" and blunt with people regarding situations, as you read in the characteristics of a prophet. Although I have inadvertently hurt some people along the way, my intentions were honestly pure in having a sincere desire to see them surrender their lives to Jesus and grow spiritually. Nevertheless, this is an area that God has and continues to help me in.

The life of an individual mantled in the prophetic office can often be lonely. However, there is joy and fulfillment in being used by God to walk in one's purpose, which includes, exhorting, admonishing, edifying, and declaring the Word of God to His people.

The role of a Christian prophet is demanding because it requires responsibility and vigilance. A prophet has five main functions: to receive and proclaim the Word of God; to actively seek out God's will and His Word; to "stir up" their gift; to "watch over" the word given and see it acted upon and fulfilled; and to intercede before God on behalf of the church. Having an immediate and obedient response to the Holy Spirit is a crucial aspect of prophetic ministry. One might be prompted to speak a message, perform a prophetic action, or even to refrain from speaking for a particular duration of time. Ezekiel was commanded by the Lord to warn the people in His name, whenever he heard a word from on high (Ezekiel 3:17).

Prophets must be responsible for continuously placing themselves in the presence of God in efforts to receive a word of direction and guidance, encouragement or rebuke. Prophets should be rightly looked to for a word from the Lord. When the people of God gather together in corporate worship, prophets often produce inspired prayer or song, or words of improvement, encouragement, or consolation, as noted in 1 Corinthians 14:3 (Yocum, 2022). Moreover, prophets generally have a spiritual stance of readiness to minister to God's people by speaking directly on His behalf. In what ways has a prophet of God spoken into your life? Do you operate in the prophetic anointing? Continue to study the Word of God and understand more about this spiritual gift and others so that you can ultimately grow in your purpose.

CHAPTER TEN

Restored Confidence

I believe that, overall, God has really and truly blessed me to have a wonderful childhood! Again, I was not perfect, nor was *everything* in my life perfect from day to day. Nevertheless, I am grateful for having had the opportunity to enjoy so many things that come with the innocence of youth (ie, outdoor adventures, imaginative explorations, riding bikes, playing with barbie dolls, watching cartoons and Disney movies, wanting for nothing, and having feelings of safety and security, etc). My parents were instrumental in ensuring that this was always the case for my siblings and me. They worked hard, and made so *many* sacrifices for us growing up, and they *still* find ways to be a blessing to each of us in our adulthood.

During my awkward adolescent years while growing up in ministry, it wasn't long before I learned just how much of a *peculiar* person I was. In 1 Peter 2: 9, we hear this terminology used to describe the people of God. The word peculiar here is most commonly assumed that it means odd or strangely different, as most Born-Again Christians are viewed as being. However, the word peculiar in this passage means belonging exclusively to an individual, distinct and set apart. That is why this verse declares that we are *chosen*, *royal* and *holy*; because this is who God has created us to be and through His infinite love for us, we uniquely belong to *Him* alone.

So, when I became filled with the Holy Spirit with the evidence of speaking in tongues as a freshman in high school, my Mother *consistently* reminded me of this fact. Through her lovingly praying for me and reminding me of who I was in Christ, she helped me so often through numerous negative feelings of inadequacies and self-doubt. Likewise, my Dad has always encouraged me and taught me to have self-confidence and believe in myself, while believing in the power of God at work through me.

During adolescent years, children frequently experience a plethora of physical, social, emotional, intellectual, psychological, and spiritual changes. So, I am *truly* grateful for my father and mother, who covered me in prayer, and wrapped me in love and support. By my parents doing this,

I was able to maintain a reasonable level of confidence and operate as the Lord would have me to from day to day. I did not realize until years later that my parents' care and compassion for me was my first example of an extension of Father God's love for me through Jesus Christ.

As I moved into adulthood, I experienced various changes between moving from my parents' home to other states and back, obtaining college degrees, the commencement of marriage and family, job changes, church membership shifts, etcetera and so forth. In the midst of all these occurrences, I cannot say that lack of confidence and self-doubt never crept in. On the contrary, I dealt with these particular enemies to my purpose quite regularly. Although my parents were always either a phone call, a few feet, or a few miles away, and even though they still poured into me and spoke life over me, there was now a difference in how I was able to respond to the Word of God. I began to really understand that I could no longer rely on *just* the comfort, prayers and encouragement of my parents, but I needed to *fully* lean and depend on Jesus to see me through every transition, every circumstance, and every obstacle.

My Mom and Dad did as they were charged to do, which was to raise me in the ways of God[17]. Even if they hadn't, because I knew the Lord Jesus Christ for myself, it was *my* responsibility to fully mature in all areas and be able to stand on my own two (spiritual) feet. We so often reference the Apostle Paul's words in First Corinthians 13, saying "when I was a child, I spoke like a child, thought like a child, and reasoned like a child. When I became an adult, I no longer used childish ways" (v.13 NOG). This verse is usually used in reference to our natural human behaviors, and how we respond throughout our early ages and stages of development. Nevertheless, this verse can also be applicable to many of us, in the context that our spiritual walk and deepening of our spiritual maturity (which for some, their growth from milk to meat [foundational to in-depth understanding])[18], *may* not necessarily align with their biological maturity.

---

[17] Proverbs 22: 6 (AMP)-" Train up a child in the way he should go [teaching him to seek God's wisdom and will for his abilities and talents], Even when he is old, he will not depart from it."

[18] I Corinthians 3: 1-3a (TLB)-" Dear brothers, I have been talking to you as though you were still just babies in the Christian life who are not following the Lord but your own desires; I cannot talk to you as I would to healthy Christians who are filled with the Spirit. I have had to feed you with milk and not with solid food because you couldn't digest anything stronger. And even now you still have

For me, I had reached a modicum of spiritual depth at a young age. Nevertheless, with the vicissitudes of life, came a deeper understanding of who God really is, which strengthened my relationship with Him. While I was in my "Patmos" experience, as discussed in chapter five, and even in recent years, I have had to wage spiritual warfare against the temptation to remain in a state of depression, losing sight of who I am in Christ. A few years ago, I had a very unfortunate situation happen to me at work that caused me to have a permanent partial disability in my right arm and right hip. The incident was very traumatic which not only affected my physical body, but my emotional state of being as well.

As a result, I was diagnosed with anxiety and had to be placed on medication to manage it. Of course, still trusting and believing God for total healing and declaring victory over my life, in His sovereignty, He brings about healing in various ways, including medical intervention. Moreover, I have had to talk myself out of bouts of negativity and

---

to be fed on milk. For you are still only baby Christians, controlled by your own desires, not God's."

encourage myself, which has helped me to have restored confidence in Christ. I could not be pulled out of this in the same manner in which I was when I was an adolescent. I had to wage war by *myself* and rejoice in advance for victory and triumph over it. However, The Message Bible translation of Philippians 3: 12-14 captures my sentiments on where I am at present with these aforementioned difficulties. Like the Apostle Paul, "**I'm** not saying that I have this all together, that I have it made. But I am well on my way, reaching out for Christ, who has so wondrously reached out for me. Friends, don't get me wrong: By no means do I count myself an expert in all of this, but I've got my eye on the goal, where God is beckoning us onward—to Jesus. I'm off and running, and I'm not turning back."

CHAPTER ELEVEN

You Better Believe It
(Trust God at His Word
and receive everything that He says about you)

Have you ever been nervous or uncertain about an attempt to do something new that you've never done before? Maybe it was preparing a big meal or new dish for your family that you haven't cooked before. Perhaps you decided to plan an event, bake a creatively professional-looking cake, build something, or complete a home improvement project. In the age of Google, Pinterest, YouTube, and TikTok hacks, you can pretty much look up detailed instructions and examples of how to do virtually *anything.* Even if you're afraid to join the growing number of "Pinterest Fails," at least you put forth the effort and *did* it! And for many of you, perhaps you were actually very pleasantly surprised by the outcome! It was simple, you followed the instructions, and it produced the intended result!

On several occasions throughout my adulthood, I have been faithful in following a basic Biblical principle, and yet, whenever I see the result of my obedience, I am astounded…tremendously grateful, yet amazed at how awesome God is, and how He is faithful to His Word!! So, what is this principle I'm speaking of? I'm talking about the principle of giving.

I have always been a cheerful, generous giver. I pay my tithes off of the gross of my increase, and I give offerings on top of my tithe. I do my best to be a blessing to others, even in seasons of having minimal to give. But one thing is for certain. I am truly a witness to the fact that God's Kingdom principle of giving through His law of reciprocity[19] *works*! As a result, countless times, I have received checks in the mail, direct deposits into my bank account, people tucking some money in my hand desiring to be a blessing, and seeing debts canceled! In those times of receiving unexpected blessings, I would be lying if I said that I have never been stressed out, and worried about where the money was going to come from to take care of certain bills, purchase groceries,

---

[19] Luke 6: 38 (KJV)-" Give, and it shall be given unto you; good measure, pressed down, and shaken together, and running over, shall men give into your bosom. For with the same measure that ye mete withal it shall be measured to you again."

buy necessities, etc. But, every single time, God has come through in His perfect timing!

Of course, I have had to learn to have some wisdom and discretion when it comes to my proclivity in being generous. I have been taken advantage of, taken for granted, and I have been walked over and blind sighted by individuals that gleaned and took everything that they could get from me (figuratively and quite *literally*...I'm talking, to the point of stealing). I have even experienced either women acting *like* me, and/or people taking my ideas, work and efforts and using it as their own, for their own advantage. And these were all *saved* and Godly people! But because I was kind, meek and mild-mannered, they did these things to me. Nevertheless, *they* will have to account for their actions and be dealt with by the Holy Spirit. Ultimately, I have learned to demonstrate generosity with wisdom and discern whether or not to withhold ideas, resources and information as needed.

But maybe giving (tithes and offerings) is not something that comes easily to you, and that's ok. It is something that I strongly advise that you begin doing, which is what God admonishes us to do (see Malachi 3: 8-18). Nevertheless, whatever it is that you find easy for you to do, or at least anticipate that you will receive *some* derivative of that intended outcome, perhaps it is fair to surmise that if we apply this mindset to other areas of our lives, we shouldn't have any problem trusting God to see us through, in order to receive the results that we are looking for. This means that we are actually *having* the faith[20] that we say we do in order for God to move on our behalf like we know that He *will*.

I had to learn to accept this truth and apply it to other areas of my life. If I can have faith to believe that God is going to meet me at every point of need, and bless me in abundance, why has it always been so difficult to believe that if I trust in Him and not lean to my own understanding, while acknowledging Him in everything that I do, He would be bringing me from season to season, ordering my steps and allowing me to enter into the fruition of my purpose (Proverbs 3: 5-6). Beloved, don't you ever forget that God is faithful to His word. If He says He is going to do something, then He absolutely *is* going to do just that!! His

---

[20] Hebrews 11: 1(KJV)-" Now faith is the substance of things hoped for, the evidence of things not seen."

Word will not be short-changed, spoken idly or empty (Isaiah 55:11). And if He *began* the work in you, He will *COMPLETE* the work in you (Philippians 1: 6).

Alas, be not dismayed, Beloved. You are not forgotten. You are not forsaken. You have not been overlooked. You are *not* ignored. Jesus loves you, and He truly has a beautiful plan in your life, that *will* be fulfilled, all for His glory and the upbuilding of His Kingdom.

CHAPTER TWELVE

Fruition

As you might recall in the introduction of this book, I discussed a metaphorical example of how a "Coming Soon" sign that we see on a plot of land is similar to our life's purpose and how God knows the end result, even in the midst of mapping out the blueprint, the construction phase, and potential delays and missteps along the way. There are other times from day to day that we may see "Coming Soon," but the steps necessary for getting *to* "that which is to come," can take on a different arrival process.

When I lived in Los Angeles, I was able to participate in various events in the entertainment industry. On a couple of occasions, I attended movie screenings of highly anticipated films. The interesting thing about the screenings was that, although we had the opportunity to view a film that was several months from being released in theaters, it was not a complete project. Oftentimes, when movie screenings occur, either the ending of the movie is yet to be filmed, or there are a few alternate endings to the movie that *were* filmed, but not shown to the viewers participating in the screening event. After the movie, producers and directors lead focus group discussions, requesting feedback from the audience on certain aspects of the film. Questionnaires are also distributed that likewise serves as a good indicator for what the audience would like to see and what they consider to be a good ending to this particular movie. In some cases, producers may even decide to go in a completely different unplanned direction of the movie as a result of the feedback that they received from the movie screening audience. At one of the screenings that I attended, several of the actors who starred in the film were in the audience as well, and after the viewing we had the opportunity to meet them and provide them with feedback concerning the roles that they portrayed in the film. By the time I got to see these movies when they were released in theaters, it was still just as exciting to watch *again* as it was initially, because *now* I was seeing the finished product! This included more polished editing, as well as a solid ending that flowed well with the overall storyline.

Similarly, our purpose as we see it right now, is not a finished product. We may be in different phases of walking out our purpose in our lives. Some of us may very actively be at or approaching the pinnacle of our purpose. Others of us may still be trying to figure out what our purpose is, or are at the beginning stages of fulfilling it. Ultimately, God is the executive director and producer of our life. In His sovereignty, He already knows exactly how our lives will pan out. He knows what our gifts, talents, and abilities are. He knows our calling because He is the one who calls us and created us. Nevertheless, God has allowed us to be free moral agents and *choose* many aspects of our lives. The choices that we make directly impact the direction that our life goes in and either keep us in the trajectory of God's *perfect* will for us or set us on a course for His *permissive* will to occur.

Those movie producers, directors and writers really already know how they want their film to end. But many times, they allow for those whom the movie is intended for (target audiences) to give their input, which can either slightly alter the finished product or maintain the synchrony of the original plans. God knows the course of our life and everything that will happen in our lives. He knows what would happen if we chose one direction over another. He knows where we will be and how we will feel when we get there. God knows *everything*. Sometimes, we might feel like things would be so much easier if we could just get a heads up on aspects of our lives as they approach us. But, just as the Apostle Paul states, "we don't yet see things clearly. We're squinting in a fog, peering through a mist. But it won't be long before the weather clears and the sun shines bright! We'll see it all then, see it all as clearly as God sees us, knowing Him directly just as He knows us" (I Corinthians 13: 12 MSG).

A couple years ago, I was praying about what endeavors God would have me to embark upon next. There are so many skill sets, gifts, talents, and abilities that God has blessed me with. Yet, I felt as though I was just sitting on them and letting them fall by the wayside. Therefore, in the summer of 2021, God led me to start a business that incorporated these abilities that He has given me. Because I have always had a heart for helping people and want to see everyone realize their purpose and thrive in it, I birthed *Fruition Consulting, LLC*. Being a writer, a motivator, and a creator are strong suits of mine. Fruition Consulting enables me to edit or ghostwrite peoples' documents and publications. I am also able to provide professional development in the areas of cultural relevance and educational advocacy; and I am able to coordinate events for individuals and organizations, among other unique projects.

Since starting Fruition Consulting, I have had a few opportunities here and there. However, I have not yet built my business up to the magnitude of it's potential. As I am striving to ultimately walk in the fruition of my purpose, which includes the success of my business, I am doing my best to support others in doing so as well, through my God-given abilities.

As I conclude *this* book, I hope that the following reminder to myself will also encourage and strengthen somebody else. So what if I didn't marry a pastor, or that I'm not currently traveling the world with a major ministry platform? I married a wonderful man of God who has a precious anointing on his life, and my major ministry is to him and our special needs children, as well as the lives that I get to touch by being an educator. In this moment, I give the Lord thanks and praise for the blessed life that He *has* given to me. He has positioned me to be able to minister to my family (immediate and extended) and all of the individuals that I encounter on a regular basis.

Beloved, I sincerely pray that through my testimony you have read in this book, you have received renewed strength, and you are encouraged by it. Even though your life may not be going as you expected or hoped it would, and although you may feel like you are meandering through your journey with no sense of direction, remember that God sees you, and He hears the cry of your heart. He is teaching you, preparing you and pruning you so that you will be ready and equipped to be all that He has made you to be. Don't be so hard on yourself, beloved. Love yourself and be happy with who you are[21] in Christ. God never makes mistakes so don't ever think that your life is one. Moreover, I admonish you that even when the road gets bumpy and foggy at times, don't give up. *Walk* in the *FRUITION* of your purpose!

---

[21] See Appendix D.

APPENDICES

APPENDIX A

Daily Confession

From God's Mouth to Kamilah's Ears 2/14/16

This year, my faith is renewed, my hope is restored and I will experience the love of God. I am accepted, approved, annointed, and appointed by God. My life has value and meaning.

I am pure, I am holy, and I am God's woman.

Love is not physical, sexual, mental, or emotional abuse. God will keep me from accepting abuse as love. I am loved by God, and I am worthy of R E A L love. My past depiction of love does not hinder my future bestowal of love, because at present, I realize that Jesus loves me.

JESUS already approved me. My affirmation and validation comes from HIM!

God thank you for refining me in a state of motivation, determination, preparation, and focus. I bless Your name, forevermore.

"I've been wounded, but I'm healed. My heart has been broken, but I'm mended. I've given up my body to harm and destruction, but I call my parts back to wholeness and reclaim my body because it is a temple of the Holy Spirit. I've been weary, but I have joy and strength. I've messed up, but God is cleaning me up. I've been disappointed, but I have hope. I am a woman of God. I am loved by God. I have value and my life has meaning. I have purpose and destiny. I am someone unique, and special, and precious in the sight of God. My past does not determine my future. My heartaches were only a set-up for my blessings, strengths, and successes. I am a child of God. I have virtue, integrity and I am upright. I am pleasing in the sight of God because He made me fearfully and wonderfully. I AM HIS and God is Mine!"

APPENDIX B

"Best Thing That Ever Happened"
by Fred Hammond

This Gift to you I bring, a simple offering
Of praise to you I sing
My grateful heart today, with joy it gives you thanks
You're the truth that lights my way

And with all my gratitude I lift my hands and worship
you
All this love from my heart to your ears
I just wanna say you're the best thing that happened
to me

I'm here with you, where I wanna be
It's clear to see, you're the best thing that happened
to me
You gave your life, just to rescue me
It's clear to see, you're the best thing that happened
to me

As loving as you are, you took my broken heart
And held it in your hand.
You're healing and touch was there, to show me that
you cared
Don't even live again (or so we can live again)

I'm here with you, where I wanna be
It's clear to see you're the best thing that happened
to me
You gave your life, just to rescue me
It's clear to see you're the best thing

One thing I know is true, falling in love with you
Is the best thing I've done
And my life has never been the same!
And with all of my heart I wanna say!

You're the best thing!
You are the best thing…!

As long as there exists a day and night
You will always be the best thing in my life…

APPENDIX C

Christine Pembleton
Lord, I'm Ready to Be a Wife: Helping You Go From Single
to Married God's Way

4.4 ★★★★☆ 16

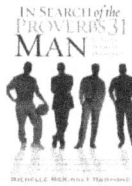

APPENDIX D

Happy Being Me
By Donald Lawrence

Looking back on

When I started

Had a lot of sun

And a lot of rain,

I've had some joy

And been broken hearted.

But now that doesn't ...mean a thing

I'm living for the joy and laughter

I'm learning from my

Befores and after's

All in all, it's been cool

His grace it brought me through

I'm so happy being me

Ohhh

So happy being me, I'm regretting nothing

Bout me

Ohhh

To busy living life giving love... freely

I'm so happy being me

Stop looking back for your beginnings.

All those broken dreams

That went down stream.

As we grow

We live and know.

FRUITION

Some things were never
meant to be

But everything

That you've been
through

God designed

Just to bless you

That's why he

Gives us memories

To lead us to our victory

I'm so happy loving me

Ohhh

So happy being me, I'm
regretting nothing

Bout me

Ohhh

To busy living life giving
love... freely

I'm

So happy being me

All of life's

Hidden treasures

I'm enjoying

Nothing but pleasure

We

Could never replace his
love (no we cant no we
cant)

But the sun light leads
us to a place

And the moon light
keeps us in his grace

Ohhh how how yea
nanana ohhh heee
ohhhh

No one else I would
rather be

Ohhhh

Ohhh, so happy being
me

I'm regretting nothing

Bout me

Ohh I'm

To busy living life giving
love... freely

I'm

So happy being me

So happy being me

I'm regretting nothing

Bout me

Come on ladies say it
with us... to busy

To busy living life giving
love... freely

I'm

So happy being me

Yes I am
So happy being me
No one else I'd rather
be
So happy being me
Yes I am oh
So happy being me
Ohhh
So happy being me

APPENDIX E

Daily Affirmation for Kids
by: Kamilah Ellis

"You're strong and triumphant and you're victorious. You're more than a conqueror and you're an overcomer. You're blessed, you're loved, you're gifted, you're anointed, and you are healed. You're covered by the Blood of Jesus.

No weapon that is formed against you shall prosper. You stand on the Word of God, and you live out of the mouth of God. You are who God says you are; and God says that you're His chosen vessel. You are a chosen generation, a royal priesthood, an holy nation, and a peculiar people, and you do show forth the praises of God who has called you out of darkness, and into His marvelous light.

You're fearfully and wonderfully made. You are the righteousness of God. You're a friend of God. You're loved of God. You're the head and not the tail. You're above and not beneath. You're the lender and not the borrower.

Good night (insert child(ren)'s name(s)). Be a good boy/girl. Have a blessed and restful night. Follow Christ."

APPENDIX F

10 Type Spiritual Gifts Strengths and Weaknesses:

Spiritual Gift	Strengths	Weaknesses
Prophecy	Clear perception of truth, ability to convey messages from God	May come across as blunt or insensitive, potential for pride
Teaching	Effective communication of knowledge, ability to explain complex concepts	Can become overly intellectual, may neglect personal relationships
Exhortation	Encouragement of others, ability to motivate and inspire	Can be overly optimistic, may avoid confronting difficult issues
Giving	Generosity, willingness to bless others	Struggle with maintaining personal boundaries, may enable unhealthy behavior
Leading	Visionary thinking, strong organizational skills	Can struggle with delegation, may become overly controlling
Mercy	Compassion, sensitivity to the needs of others	Can become overly empathetic, may neglect personal well-being
Healing	Ability to bring physical, emotional, or spiritual healing	May struggle with setting limits, can become overwhelmed by needs
Discernment	Deep spiritual insight, ability to discern truth from falsehood	Can become overly critical, may struggle with trust
Tongues	Ability to communicate in unknown languages, often used in prayer	Can be misused or misunderstood, may cause confusion or division
Interpretation of Tongues	Ability to interpret the messages of those speaking in tongues	Can be misused or misunderstood, may be limited in application

10 Type Spiritual Gifts Strengths and Weaknesses:

APPENDIX G

Understanding the Spiritual Gift of Prophecy

General Characteristics	Strengths	Weaknesses
A prophet's basic motivational drive is to apply the Word of God to a situation so that sin is exposed and relationships are restored. Prophets might be considered the "trumpets" of the Body of Christ who sound the alarm in the face of sin and compromise. • A prophet calls attention to sin and wrong attitudes. • The prophet is passionate about exposing sin, but not primarily so that sinners can be punished. Rather, he is passionate about exposing sin so that *truth can be revealed and fellowship with God can be restored.* • A prophet has a God-given ability to sense when compromises are being made, and his nature demands that action be taken—something must be done. This action may take the form of an overt protest or confrontation, or it may take the form of a conversation or correspondence. • For a prophet, any solution that involves compromise is unacceptable. • For the prophet, to observe or discern sin and say nothing is, of itself, sin. Naturally, knowing that a prophet has this perspective tends to make some of us feel intimidated or uncomfortable around them—even when we are guiltless! The prophet's abhorrence of sin can easily be viewed as a judgmental spirit, and no one wants to be the object of that judgment. • The prophet often displays the spiritual gift of discerning of spirits; he is able to discern true motives as the Holy Spirit gives him divine insights. As a general rule, the prophet is more interested in whether or not the heart is pure than whether or not the activity in question is acceptable. • Prophets are usually outspoken, sometimes brash; they tell it like it is. • They tend to see issues as "black or white," not "gray."	• A prophet is confident in his use of Scripture, because he regards Scripture as the only source of truth. • A mature prophet easily discerns hypocrisy, because God has gifted him to discern Truth. • He is usually more teachable than others, especially when discipline or correction is required. When a wise prophet is confronted with his sin, he sees it as God sees it and consequently is crushed (if he is walking in the Spirit and not in the flesh). • The prophet accepts absolutes easily. The rest of us try to explain them away; prophets simply take God at His Word. • He is not easily swayed by emotions. • A prophet has a deep capacity to trust God, based on what God has promised. This is the prophet's attitude: "If it's right, do it. Trust God for the outcome—it's His responsibility."	• A prophet's need to be "painfully truthful" may result in insensitivity or harshness. • Prophets often have little sympathy and patience with people who do not respond objectively. • A prophet's sense of conviction may tempt him or her to become intolerant or prideful. • Because of the prophet's deep consciousness of sin, he sometimes seems to have a negative, "gloomy" approach to life.

REFERENCES

ABC News. (2018, May 23). Miracle babies: Helping parents of premature babies feel less alone. *ABC News*. https://www.abc.net.au/news/2018-05-23/miracle-babies-foundation-helps-parents-feel-less-alone/9762488?utm_campaign=abc_news_web&utm_content=link&utm_medium=content_shared&utm_source=abc_news_web

Angel baby - | Oxford English Dictionary. (n.d.). https://www.oed.com/search/dictionary/?scope=Entries&q=angel+baby

Council, F. C. (2017, August 3). How To Define Your Defining Moments. *Forbes*. https://www.forbes.com/sites/forbescoachescou

ncil/2017/08/03/how-to-define-your-defining-
moments/?sh=46bc9ae225d0

*Fred Hammond - Best Thing That Ever Happened
lyrics | Lyrics.com.* (n.d.).
https://www.lyrics.com/lyric/17706661/Fred+H
ammond/Best+Thing+That+Ever+Happened

Fruition Definition & Meaning | Dictionary.com.
(2021). In *Dictionary.com.*
https://www.dictionary.com/browse/fruition

Kruger, M. (2017, June 13). Stirring the Nest: An Eagle's
lesson on God's Love. *The Gospel Coalition.*
https://www.thegospelcoalition.org/blogs/melissa-
kruger/why-did-moses-describe-god-like-an-eagle-
4-reasons/

Parker, D. (2023, June 8). *Spiritual Gifts Strengths
And Weaknesses: Understanding!* SpiritualAsk.
Retrieved November 18, 2023, from

https://spiritualask.com/spiritual-gifts-strengths-and-weaknesses/

Regan, S., & Hallett, K. (2022, June 30). *7 Signs You're An Ambivert, The Introvert-Extrovert Mix | mindbodygreen*. MindBodyGreen. Retrieved November 13, 2023, from https://www.mindbodygreen.com/articles/ambivert-meaning-and-signs

Rickroehm, V. a. P. B. (2011, January 28). *What is the Adamic nature?* ChristianBlessings. https://ptl2010.com/2011/01/29/what-is-the-adamic-nature/

Role of a prophet. (n.d.). Scribd. https://www.scribd.com/document/341412921/Role-of-a-Prophet

Rowley, L. (2022, September 21). *The Purpose Driven Life Summary - Four minute books*. Four

Minute Books.

https://fourminutebooks.com/the-purpose-

driven-life-summary/

Tarbox, P. (2015, June 3). *10 Indicators A Spirit of*

Rejection Is Tormenting You - Above & Beyond

Christian Counseling. Above & Beyond

Christian Counseling.

https://aandbcounseling.com/10-indicators-

spirit-of-rejection-tormenting/

WebMD Editorial Contributors. (2021, March 14).

What is a rainbow baby? WebMD.

https://www.webmd.com/baby/what-is-a-

rainbow-

baby#:~:text=A%20rainbow%20baby%20is%2

0a,ectopic%20pregnancy%2C%20or%20blighte

d%20ovum.

What is the spiritual gift of prophecy? (n.d.). Institute
in Basic Life Principles. Retrieved November
21, 2023, from https://iblp.org/what-spiritual-
gift-prophecy/

What was the "Most Holy Place" or the "Holy of Holies"?
(n.d.). CompellingTruth.org.
https://www.compellingtruth.org/holy-of-
holies.html

Yocum, B. (2022, August 3). *The Gift of Prophecy:
The Prophet's Role – Living Bulwark*. Living
Bulwark. Retrieved November 21, 2023, from
https://livingbulwark.net/the-gift-of-prophecy-
the-prophets-role%EF%BF%BC/

NOTES

FRUITION

FRUITION

www.ingramcontent.com/pod-product-compliance
Lightning Source LLC
Chambersburg PA
CBHW060403090426
42734CB00011B/2245